Friends
Are the
Heart of
Christmas

We wish to thank Susan Polis Schutz for permission to reprint the following poem that appears in this publication: "You're One of the Best Friends I've Ever Known." Copyright © 1986 by Stephen Schutz and Susan Polis Schutz. All rights reserved.

ISBN: 978-1-59842-902-2

■ and Blue Mountain Press are registered in U.S. Patent and Trademark Office. Certain trademarks are used under license.

Acknowledgments appear on the last page.

Printed in China.
First Printing: 2015

♻ This book is printed on recycled paper.

This book is printed on paper that has been specially produced to be acid free (neutral pH) and contains no groundwood or unbleached pulp. It conforms with the requirements of the American National Standards Institute, Inc., so as to ensure that this book will last and be enjoyed by future generations.

Blue Mountain Arts, Inc.

P.O. Box 4549, Boulder, Colorado 80306

Friends Are the Heart of Christmas

...and I'm So Lucky to Call You Mine

A Blue Mountain Arts® Collection

Edited by Patricia Wayant

Blue Mountain Press™

Boulder, Colorado

At Christmas and All Year Through...
I Treasure Our Friendship

I tried to think of something
I could give you this Christmas
that would signify all you mean
    to me.
It had to be something very special
because that's what you are.
It had to be something that
    would last,
just as our friendship has all
    these years.
It had to be something that
    would make you feel good,
because that's how I feel
    anytime we're together.

It had to be a reminder of
    the good times we've had,
something that would connect you to me
    in memories.
It had to be filled with hope
and faith in the future
and dreams just waiting to come true.

If I could wrap up all my memories of us
together with the laughter, the secrets,
and the comforting and encouraging
    words we've shared,
I'd sprinkle it all with faith,
stir in a promise of forever,
    and seal it with love to send to you.
Because all along I knew
    that there is no greater gift
than the wonderful friendship we share,
and all I can ever hope to do
    is give it back to you.

— Barbara Cage

I'm So Lucky to Have a Friend like You

One of the best feelings in the whole world comes from being a friend… and having a friend in return.

I wouldn't trade my friendship with you for anything… because I know that nothing else could ever begin to bring me the contentment, the wonderful craziness, the support and the caring, the laughter, the understanding, and all the thousands of things that we share together.

One of the sweetest feelings in the whole world comes from knowing that everything we share — and the joy that graces our lives — will warm our hearts forever, in all the days ahead.

For no matter how far apart
our paths may wander,
and no matter how long it's been,
it's so great to know that…

you and I will always be
the closest and
dearest of friends.

— Lorrie Westfall

Friends Are the Heart of Christmas

*F*riends are such an important part of the season. They're in the moments that make you smile and the happy memories imprinted on your heart.

Friends always seem to notice when you need a little help and will share a hug, a smile, or a prayer. When the world around you is upside down, friends make it right. They see things on a deeper level. They can look right into your eyes and know what you're feeling. They are true angels — no wings or halos required.

Friends have too many special qualities to count and so many ways of always being there for you. When you've got a friend standing behind your dreams, anything is possible. When life sets up roadblocks, friends help you go around them. They will go to any length to see you through. They will teach you everything there is to know about caring and faith. Especially in this season of the year, friends are always where your heart is.

— Linda E. Knight

Where Does the Time Go?

The holidays seem to arrive
    more quickly each year,
and I find myself scrambling
    for every extra minute.
But when I stop to look around,
    take a deep breath
and a moment to recapture
    the spirit of the season,
I remember that this is meant
    to be a time of celebration.
Love and laughter are supposed
    to fill these days.
That's when I remember the people
    who mean so much to me —
        people like you.

The holidays are for friends like you:
wonderful souls who give of themselves
and put their energy into bringing
    happiness to others all year,
never asking for anything
    but love in return.
They are for counting blessings,
    and I certainly count you among
the most precious of mine.

— Jennifer Ellis May

What is the spirit of Christmas, you ask?

*L*et me give you the answer in a true story...

On a cold day in December, feeling especially warm in my heart for no other reason than it was the holiday season, I walked through the store sporting a big grin on my face. Though most people were far too busy going about their business to notice me, one elderly gentleman in a wheelchair brought his eyes up to meet mine as we neared each other traveling opposite directions. He slowed in passing just long enough to speak to me.

"Now that's a Christmas smile if I ever saw one," he said.

My lips stretched to their limit in response, and I thanked him for the compliment. Then we went our separate ways. But, as I thought about the man and how sweetly he'd touched me, I realized something simply wonderful! In that brief, passing interaction we'd exchanged heartfelt gifts!

And that, my friend, is the spirit of Christmas.

— Richelle E. Goodrich

Why God Made Friends...

He never intended
for us to walk alone through life —
that is why He created friends.
He places these special people
in our path to walk with us.

You and I have been friends
     for a long time.
Our hearts are interlocked,
and what we are together
makes us stronger
and helps us persevere.

Together we've tried our wings;
we've soared high and crashed,
celebrated and cried.
We've dried each other's tears
and picked up the pieces
        of broken dreams.
We've made things better
        than they were before.
It's not even so much the help
        we've given each other;
it's the absolute confidence
that we're always there —
wanting, willing, and ready to help.
Above all, friendship is a gift
        of oneself to another.
Thank you for sharing such
        a beautiful gift with me.

— Vickie M. Worsham

"That's just what good friends do"

Just like everyone else, I have times when I know that I can't do it all by myself. There are times when I need encouragement and some extra strength, a bit of wisdom, a little humor, and a lot of knowing that someone is on my side. It may be a situation that needs some gentle understanding; it might be a problem that needs to be talked out. There are so many aspects of my life that benefit tremendously by a friend — just "listening in" and then sharing insights that could only come from someone on the inside. There are times when the only thing that sees me through... is the friend I have in you.

You are the one person I know I can turn to, and I want to say that everything I have with you... you have with me. You can call on me, turn to me, and count on me to be there for you wherever, whenever. Because you so generously share the laughter, I will lovingly dry any tears. Because you so kindly believe in me, I will never stop believing in you. I will cheer you on and do whatever I can to help you reach out for your hopes and dreams. But I'll also be there to protect you, to ease any burdens, and to remind you that there are two of us to overpower any worries and chase away any fears.

When two people are as close as we are, the giving and the taking blend together into one. There's no keeping score. There's just giving more.

That's just what good friends do.

— Douglas Pagels

You're One of the Best Friends I've Ever Known

*B*est friends always
    remember so well
all the things they did together
all the subjects they discussed
all the mistakes they made
all the fun they had

Best friends always remember
how their friendship
was such a stabilizing force
during confusing times
in their lives

Best friends may have
    different lifestyles
live in different places
and interact with different people
but no matter how much
their lives may change
their friendship remains the same

I know that throughout my life
wherever I am
I will always
remember so well
and cherish our friendship
as one of the best
I have ever known

— Susan Polis Schutz

You've Given Me the Gift of True Friendship

True friendship is that unexplained heart connection between two people who enrich each other's life. They may not know exactly why they became friends, but they do know that their presence in each other's life is a gift.

True friendship is one of the most valuable treasures anyone could have. It is necessary nourishment to the heart and soul. It creates a feeling of unconditional acceptance between two people who allow each other to be themselves — just as they are.

True friends are sensitive to each other's own perceived flaws, insecurities, vanities, peculiarities, and opinions, but neither puts demands on the other to change. They just want the best for each other... always. This kind of relationship takes no effort and needs no rules.

This is our kind of friendship... the kind that exists between two people who understand each other and know how to communicate with each other — often by not saying a word.

Thanks for giving me the gift of true friendship.

— Donna Fargo

A Little Christmas Prayer I'd Love to Share with You

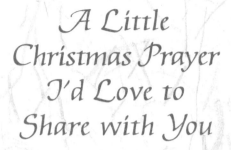

I want your life to be such
   a wonderful one.
I wish you peace,
   deep within your soul;
joyfulness in the promise
   of each new day;
stars to reach for,
   dreams to come true,
and memories more beautiful
   than words can say.

I wish you friends close at heart,
   even over the miles;
loved ones — the best treasures
   we're blessed with;
present moments to live in,
   one day at a time.

I wish you serenity, with its wisdom;
    courage, with its strength;
and new beginnings, to give life a
    chance to really shine.

I wish you understanding —
    of how special you really are;
a journey, safe from the storms and
    warmed by the sun;
a path to wonderful things;
an invitation, to the abundance
    life brings;
and an angel watching over,
    for all the days to come.

— Douglas Pagels

The Blessings of Christmas

Christmas is the time of year
when we look back on
all the blessings we have received.
The greatest blessings
are not ones of monetary value.
They aren't our possessions.
The true blessing in life
is the love of family and friends —
the people who are by our side
through the ups and downs of life,
through struggles and celebrations.
They are the people who are with us
throughout the journey of life,
no matter what surprises may come up.
These are the people we can count on…
people like you.

— April Aragam

Christmas is a time to reflect on what is most important in our lives. I am reminded of all your kindness and warmth — and the beautiful ways that you have touched my life. I count my lucky stars every day knowing that we have such an extraordinary friendship.

— Peggy Wharton-Goroly

How to Keep Christmas in Your Heart...

1. *Shine...* with your God-given talents.
2. *Sparkle...* with interest when you listen to others.
3. *Twinkle...* with a sense of humor, and you'll never take life too seriously.
4. *Sing...* to keep up your spirits.
5. *Pray...* and you'll know you're never alone.
6. *Unwrap...* your dreams and make them happen.

7. *Celebrate…* your every step to success.
8. *Decorate…* your own space and make it your peaceful retreat.
9. *Play…* with passion after you work hard.
10. *Exchange…* your doubts for hopes; your frowns for smiles.
11. *Make…* cookies, friends, happiness.
12. *Believe…* in the spirit of Santa Claus and in your power to make the world a better place.

— Jacqueline Schiff

A Little Holiday Advice...

Enjoy your life!
Laugh a lot. Love a lot.
Listen to your heart,
and follow where it leads you.
Do what you love.
Love yourself,
and share that love with others.
This is the way that we truly
make a difference,
add our beauty to the world,
and give something precious
to ourselves and others.

— Donna Newman

Christmas Cheer Recipe

Take a bushel of tinsel, sprinkle well
throughout the house.
Add two dozen stars and one graceful
Christmas tree.
Take a generous spray of mistletoe, an armload of holly,
and a full measure of snow laid in curved hills
along the windowsills.
Toss in a Christmas carol, and season well with
goodwill and friendly laughter.
Light the candles, "one for adoration,
two for celebration."
Let the first burn brightly, and may those you
love be near.
The yield: *one happy Christmas.*

— Clementine Paddleford

This Christmas, I Want to Thank You

I want to let you know how much I appreciate all the gifts you have shared with me throughout our many years of friendship.

Thank you for... your gift of understanding when nobody else understood; your gift of sunshine when I saw only dark clouds above my head; your gift of forgiveness when I hurt or offended you.

Thank you for... your gift of hope when I thought there was no way out of my difficulties; your gift of laughter when my heart was about to cry; your gift of faithfulness when my other friends could not be found.

Most of all, thank you for the ever-present gift of your love — a gift I never take for granted, because you are my friend.

— Pamela A. Babusci

You Show the Real Meaning of Friendship

Friendship cannot be measured by years. It cannot be measured by how often you talk or how close you live. Friendship cannot be measured by what you do for each other. In fact, true friendship cannot be measured at all.

True friendship is confirmed through the kindness and compassion that is shared between two people. It emerges when nurtured with warmth and empathy. True friends are not afraid to be judged and can speak openly and freely. True friends do not always agree, but they do accept each other's position. Separation and time will not damage the relationship but only form a stronger bond.

Not everyone encounters a true friend in their lifetime. We frequently grow in and out of friends over the years. Often we have many close friends, some of them lasting decades, but rarely do we find a real inner-reaching friend. In you I have a true friend.

I know this because in my life there is a space that you have filled from the beginning. I hope I always fulfill our friendship for you as you have for me. I want to be here for you always, because a true friend may only pass our way once.

— Amanda-Lea Thoreck

You're
My Friend
for Life

*W*hen two people have shared
as much as you and I have;
when they've opened up
their hearts,
shared their dreams,
thoughts, and fears;
when two people
know each other well enough
to know if sadness
is hiding behind a smile
or if happiness is
glowing in the other's eyes…

when they've shared so many laughs
and when each other's pain
at times has triggered tears;
when two people believe in each other
and are always sincere to each other;
when they have trusted each other
with the truth that lies within —
then you can be sure
that they're friends for life…
just like you and me.

— Zoe Dellous

At Christmas, I Feel Truly Blessed to Call You My Friend

Christmas is the perfect time
to reflect on all our blessings.
The true blessings in life
are the people who inspire us
to live a better life,
love us unconditionally,
and make us smile
even when times are tough.
You are one of the greatest blessings
in my life.

In this holiday season,
I celebrate you
and the joy, optimism, and love
that you bring to my life,
and I wish you a Christmas
that reminds you
just how special you are
to everyone around you.

— April Aragam

*My Dear
Friend,
I Wish You
a Wonderful
Christmas*

At this beautiful time of year,
I especially want to let you know
how very dear you are to me
and how fondly I hold you
in my heart.

The friendship we share
is a precious gift we continue
to give each other,
and the more we give,
   the more it grows.

The time we spend together,
the conversations only we can follow,
and the unspoken understanding
we are so blessed to share
are the greatest gifts
anyone can give or receive.

Things can be lost or stolen or broken;
our friendship cannot.
I wish for you the most valuable
    gifts of the season —
joy, peace, happiness,
    time with friends and family,
and the luminous light of love —
because you are one of the bright lights
that graces my life every day.

— Deborah Correia McDaniels

ACKNOWLEDGMENTS

We gratefully acknowledge the permission granted by the following authors and authors' representatives to reprint poems or excerpts from their publications:

Linda E. Knight for "Friends Are the Heart of Christmas." Copyright © 2015 by Linda E. Knight. All rights reserved.

Richelle E. Goodrich, www.Harrowbeth.com, for "What is the spirit of Christmas, you ask?" from SMILE ANYWAY: QUOTES, VERSE, & GRUMBLINGS FOR EVERY DAY OF THE YEAR. Copyright © 2013 by Richelle E. Goodrich. Reprinted by permission. All rights reserved.

PrimaDonna Entertainment Corp. for "You've Given Me the Gift of True Friendship" by Donna Fargo. Copyright © 2003 by PrimaDonna Entertainment Corp. All rights reserved.

April Aragam for "At Christmas, I Feel Truly Blessed to Call You My Friend." Copyright © 2015 by April Aragam. All rights reserved.

A careful effort has been made to trace the ownership of selections used in this anthology in order to obtain permission to reprint copyrighted material and give proper credit to the copyright owners. If any error or omission has occurred, it is completely inadvertent, and we would like to make corrections in future editions provided that written notification is made to the publisher:

BLUE MOUNTAIN ARTS, INC., P.O. Box 4549, Boulder, Colorado 80306.